Desktop-as-a-Service (DaaS)

Nutanix Special Edition

by Scott D. Lowe

Desktop-as-a-Service (DaaS) For Dummies®, Nutanix Special Edition

Published by
John Wiley & Sons, Inc.
111 River St.
Hoboken, NJ 07030-5774
www.wiley.com

Copyright © 2019 by John Wiley & Sons, Inc., Hoboken, New Jersey

No part of this publication may be reproduced, stored in a retrieval system or transmitted in any form or by any means, electronic, mechanical, photocopying, recording, scanning or otherwise, except as permitted under Sections 107 or 108 of the 1976 United States Copyright Act, without the prior written permission of the Publisher. Requests to the Publisher for permission should be addressed to the Permissions Department, John Wiley & Sons, Inc., 111 River Street, Hoboken, NJ 07030, (201) 748-6011, fax (201) 748-6008, or online at http://www.wiley.com/go/permissions.

Trademarks: Wiley, For Dummies, the Dummies Man logo, Dummies.com, and related trade dress are trademarks or registered trademarks of John Wiley & Sons, Inc. and/or its affiliates in the United States and other countries, and may not be used without written permission. Nutanix and the Nutanix logo are trademarks or registered trademarks of Nutanix. All other trademarks are the property of their respective owners. John Wiley & Sons, Inc., is not associated with any product or vendor mentioned in this book.

LIMIT OF LIABILITY/DISCLAIMER OF WARRANTY: THE PUBLISHER AND THE AUTHOR MAKE NO REPRESENTATIONS OR WARRANTIES WITH RESPECT TO THE ACCURACY OR COMPLETENESS OF THE CONTENTS OF THIS WORK AND SPECIFICALLY DISCLAIM ALL WARRANTIES, INCLUDING WITHOUT LIMITATION WARRANTIES OF FITNESS FOR A PARTICULAR PURPOSE. NO WARRANTY MAY BE CREATED OR EXTENDED BY SALES OR PROMOTIONAL MATERIALS. THE ADVICE AND STRATEGIES CONTAINED HEREIN MAY NOT BE SUITABLE FOR EVERY SITUATION. THIS WORK IS SOLD WITH THE UNDERSTANDING THAT THE PUBLISHER IS NOT ENGAGED IN RENDERING LEGAL, ACCOUNTING, OR OTHER PROFESSIONAL SERVICES. IF PROFESSIONAL ASSISTANCE IS REQUIRED, THE SERVICES OF A COMPETENT PROFESSIONAL PERSON SHOULD BE SOUGHT. NEITHER THE PUBLISHER NOR THE AUTHOR SHALL BE LIABLE FOR DAMAGES ARISING HEREFROM. THE FACT THAT AN ORGANIZATION OR WEBSITE IS REFERRED TO IN THIS WORK AS A CITATION AND/OR A POTENTIAL SOURCE OF FURTHER INFORMATION DOES NOT MEAN THAT THE AUTHOR OR THE PUBLISHER ENDORSES THE INFORMATION THE ORGANIZATION OR WEBSITE MAY PROVIDE OR RECOMMENDATIONS IT MAY MAKE. FURTHER, READERS SHOULD BE AWARE THAT INTERNET WEBSITES LISTED IN THIS WORK MAY HAVE CHANGED OR DISAPPEARED BETWEEN WHEN THIS WORK WAS WRITTEN AND WHEN IT IS READ.

For general information on our other products and services, or how to create a custom *For Dummies* book for your business or organization, please contact our Business Development Department in the U.S. at 877-409-4177, contact info@dummies.biz, or visit www.wiley.com/go/custompub. For information about licensing the *For Dummies* brand for products or services, contact BrandedRights&Licenses@Wiley.com.

ISBN 978-1-119-59739-1 (pbk); ISBN 978-1-119-59735-3 (ebk)

Manufactured in the United States of America

10 9 8 7 6 5 4 3 2 1

Publisher's Acknowledgments

We're proud of this book and of the people who worked on it. For details on how to create a custom *For Dummies* book for your business or organization, contact info@dummies.biz or visit www.wiley.com/go/custompub. For details on licensing the *For Dummies* brand for products or services, contact BrandedRights&Licenses@Wiley.com.

Some of the people who helped bring this book to market include the following:

Project Editor: Martin V. Minner

Associate Publisher: Katie Mohr

Editorial Manager: Rev Mengle

Business Development Representative: Karen Hattan

Production Editor: Tamilmani Varadharaj

Table of Contents

Introduction

I f you have an office at work, you more than likely also have a desktop computer or a laptop, the device provided by your employer that tethers you to your job while making it possible to fulfill the expectations set forth for said job.

Over the past 25 years or more, that paradigm — the desktop or laptop sitting there on your desk — hasn't changed an awful lot. Some companies have adopted server-based computing and virtual desktop products, which you can learn about in this book, but most still just have that computer sitting on the desk.

This current model has some big drawbacks:

>> It's inefficient.

>> It's expensive.

>> Adding desktops can take a lot of time.

>> Managing and maintaining the environment is increasingly difficult.

>> Those who have undertaken virtual desktop projects have discovered that the technology has its own pitfalls, which this book discusses as well.

In recent years, a number of trends have converged, providing organizations the opportunity to massively rethink how they provide desktop services to their employees:

>> The cloud has continued its insidious penetration into all parts of IT, with its latest target being desktop computing.

>> Users have proclaimed their ownership of their own devices, sparking a trend in which they want to use their own stuff rather than the stuff given to them by the company.

>> Security concerns have skyrocketed to the top of the "We really have to look at this" list, pushing companies to realize that their desktop computing environment is leakier than a sieve.

This is where desktop-as-a-service (DaaS) jumps into the frame by helping organizations handily solve their desktop computing dilemma.

About This Book

The subject of this book is DaaS. In these chapters I regale you with tales from the dark ages of IT in which the much-lamented modern computing era was founded. I follow that up with a discussion about the cloud and the wonders that it has brought to the modern gilded age of IT. Then, I jump into a discussion of DaaS and what it can mean for you and your enterprise.

Foolish Assumptions

I'm assuming that you know a bit about computers, virtualization, and the cloud. You don't need to be a pro, but you should be able to type your full name without having to look at the keyboard. This book is written primarily for IT executives and managers such as CIOs, CTOs, IT directors, and technical managers. If you're not one of these people, that's okay. Read this book anyway because there's something for everyone!

Icons Used in This Book

Several icons appear in the margins of this book. Here's a rundown of what these icons mean.

REMEMBER

Anything that has a Remember icon is well worth committing to memory.

TECHNICAL STUFF

The Technical Stuff icon indicates extra-credit reading. You can skip it if you like (but I hope you won't).

TIP

The Tip icon points out helpful information.

WARNING

The Warning icon alerts you to risks of various kinds.

Chapter 1

The Innovation of Desktop Virtualization

Markets come and markets go. Over the past couple of decades, one market has shifted dramatically, shrinking from dozens and dozens of specialty vendors to just a few behemoths producing the vast majority of the goods in this space.

That market, the desktop computer market, includes the full spectrum of laptops and desktops that are used by corporate minions, by students in college computer labs, and by the always-cheerful folks at the department of motor vehicles.

Desktop computing may not always feel like the most exciting or vibrant aspect of your company's information technology function, but the fact remains that desktops and laptops are critical to your company's success. However, that doesn't mean that there isn't serious room for improvement.

In this chapter, you delve into the world of the desktop support model and discover the various methods by which you can provide your users with devices that enable them to access your line of business applications.

Understanding the Legacy Desktop Model

Way back in the day (and I mean *way* back), companies bought a few computers to help with things like bookkeeping and as a part of a broader management information systems strategy. Over the years, as desktop computers proliferated and were augmented by portable computers, organizations began implementing comprehensive — and expensive — hardware replacement cycles.

Expanding the application landscape

Early on, desktop computers often ran most of their applications locally, although they may still have connected to a central system, such as a mainframe or mini-computer or network server, for some of them. Under this paradigm, desktop administrators were responsible for ensuring that every computer had the requisite software installed and remained in top working condition.

As networks came on the scene and, in particular, as the Internet became the force that it now is, desktops took on a different role. Although many applications still run locally, more applications are accessed remotely. Software-as-a-service (SaaS) applications have replaced many formerly local applications, and most companies of any size have centralized data resources for which desktop computers and laptops are simply access mechanisms.

As of today, the enterprise application landscape is firmly in a hybrid scenario. Many applications remain rooted to the desktop, but a great many are now accessed with the desktop simply acting as a terminal.

Anchoring IT: How the desktop became an ecosystem

With an understanding of the application landscape, you might think that's the beginning and the end of the desktop discussion. Unfortunately, nothing could be further from the truth. Over the years, the desktop environment has become increasingly complex, with new challenges emerging at every turn.

For organizations with more than a handful of desktop computers or laptops, ongoing management of those devices can be an utter nightmare. From ensuring security to making sure everyone has the software they need, to ensuring a cohesive and simple user experience, desktop computing complexity can quickly grow out of control.

Here are some challenges:

>> **Security:** Desktops are among the primary vulnerability points in an organization, and multiple vectors can be in play. A user can fall victim to malware from an email or from an unpatched desktop software vulnerability. Perhaps a laptop user is traveling and their device is stolen, along with all of the company data it was holding.

>> **Manageability:** Keeping tabs on patches, software releases, antivirus, and a multitude of other desktop needs is a full-time job . . . literally. Larger organizations may have an army of people with desktop management software suites to make sure that the company's desktop armada is ready to do battle each day.

>> **The user experience:** Ensuring that users have complete access to the resources that they need, including locally installed software and file repositories, can be a full-time feat as well.

>> **Ongoing replacement:** Hardware wears out. New applications demand more RAM, more storage performance, and more CPU. Organizations have carefully tailored replacement cycles intended to meet the ongoing needs of applications. Every three to five years, every desktop computer in an organization is chucked into the landfill — or recycled — and replaced with a shiny new one.

>> **Capital and operational cost:** To make it all work, desktop environments carry significant capital and operational costs. You have to buy all the hardware and software and then you have to maintain it. The upfront costs every year to buy hardware can be prohibitive.

To ensure ongoing security, compliance, and manageability for the desktop environment, companies have built entire departments and systems around these devices. They deploy tools that reduce the operational burden of managing dozens, hundreds, or thousands of devices. These tools require expertise to operate, and managing a comprehensive desktop environment requires ongoing diligence.

REMEMBER

Of course, you can find ways to mitigate some of these threats. For example, if your company requires you to encrypt your laptop, and you lose the device, the potential for a breach of company data plummets, but you still have the potential for losing any data that was stored locally. So, although you have ways to reduce the risk, you can't completely eliminate risk in a traditional desktop scenario.

Discovering the VDI Landscape

Virtualization. Perhaps you've heard of it? It was all the rage for servers back in the early part of the century and, today, it's become the de facto standard method by which new workloads are deployed in an organization.

Over the years, many services have been deployed to try to ease the desktop management burden for administrators, provide improved levels of flexibility for users, and improve the overall security of the entire environment.

The following sections describe the efforts to date and provide an overview of the good and not-so-good, where applicable, about each one.

Server-based computing with Terminal Services

One of the earliest attempts to solve the desktop problem came by taking a cue from the past with server-based computing. Essentially, servers are turned into centralized locations from which to run applications. Terminal Services — sometimes referred to as a *session virtualization technology* — converts desktop computers, laptops, and other devices with terminal software into dumb terminals. With Terminal Services, the heavy lifting around processing, RAM, and storage is handled at the server and the clients are nothing but windows into that environment. They get screens from the server and are the user's input device. With Terminal Services, your end-user devices can be incredibly lightweight.

This deployment model has great benefits for IT. Rather than install applications across thousands of computers, they can be installed on the Terminal Server just once. Now, there's just one copy of an application to maintain.

TECHNICAL STUFF

On the downside, these environments aren't always ideal for graphics-intensive applications or applications that require specialized hardware. Moreover, some applications simply won't operate in this kind of shared environment or carry additional licensing costs to do so. With Microsoft, some tricky licensing considerations can surround Terminal Services, and it isn't hard to get yourself unintentionally out of compliance.

Application virtualization

Virtualization didn't stop at the Terminal Server. Application virtualization works to solve the desktop application from a different angle. When you install an application the traditional way, it installs a bunch of hooks into the operating system to make various aspects of the application work. However, the desktop environment is often not static, meaning that a lot of variance exists in the hardware, operating systems, and applications in use across the entire desktop fleet.

Unfortunately, some applications simply won't work in some environments, whether it's because of a hardware issue, an operating system incompatibility, or a conflict with another installed application. Desktop fleet variance creates an inconsistent environment into which to deploy applications, significantly increasing the challenge associated with managing these systems.

REMEMBER

This is where application virtualization comes in. With application virtualization, a single copy of an application is packaged up into a wrapper that includes all of the underlying hooks that are necessary for the application to operate. The wrapper essentially emulates the integration points from an operating system environment that is friendly to the application. This approach has multiple benefits:

>> One application can run alongside another otherwise incompatible app because each is packaged in its own independent wrapper that isolates it from other apps.

>> Applications can be more easily deployed because there is one true master image for each application and it installs across all devices.

>> Managing the desktop environment is less complex.

Application virtualization tools can be used in concert with other desktop virtualization technologies, including Terminal Services and virtual desktop infrastructure (VDI).

The benefits of this technology are clear, but there are downsides, too. Although it eases the complexity in the overall desktop environment, it adds a need for specialized skills in IT. You need someone who understands these tools inside and out. That can get expensive. Moreover, this technology is another layer of the desktop onion that has to be peeled away and paid for. The tools may require separate licensing fees, so they add to the direct costs of the desktop environment.

Virtual desktop infrastructure

Virtual desktop infrastructure (VDI) is a great way to centralize and improve the overall efficiency of a desktop environment. Essentially, just as you do with your servers, you virtualize desktops and run them from the data center.

VDI provides an organization with some serious benefits, too. Believe it or not, one of the biggest benefits is security. With VDI, user desktops run inside the confines of your nice, cozy, safe data center. Users access their desktops through a client. Therefore, no actual data leaves your data center. Users don't store company data on local devices that they then leave at the local watering hole. It's a match made in security heaven.

VDI also provides eminent flexibility for your users because they can access their desktops anytime, anywhere, and from any device as long as they have an appropriate client. From an application perspective, VDI is super easy to deal with because every desktop is identical. The underlying hardware is just a virtual machine, so they're all the same. You have no more variability to deal with.

TIP

Chapter 2 goes into more depth about VDI, so move ahead to that chapter if you'd like to learn more.

Desktop-as-a-service

Desktop-as-a-service (DaaS) is a relative newcomer in the virtual desktop space. Because it's the topic of the rest of this book, I'm keeping the description in this section brief.

REMEMBER

Simply put, DaaS is a desktops-in-a-box solution that typically operates in the cloud but can also be deployed in a local data center. Either way, DaaS provides desktops-as-a-service from both a technical and financial perspective. Rather than buying a bunch of hardware and software up front and cobbling it all together, you simply provision virtual desktops and start using them. It's that simple. As for payment, you pay a monthly fee per desktop in use.

So, you have no deployment beyond a few clicks of a mouse and you pay as you go per month. Super easy! Table 1-1 compares the desktop virtualization options.

TABLE 1-1 Comparing Desktop Virtualization Options

	Terminal Services	Application Virtualization	VDI	DaaS	Hybrid DaaS
Capital Expenditure	Moderate	Low	High	None	Moderate
Operational Expenditure	Moderate	Moderate	Moderate to high	High	Moderate
End-User Experience	Moderate	Moderate	Varies	Very positive	Very positive
IT Operational Impact	Moderate	Moderate	Very high	Very low	Moderate
Completeness of Solution	Moderate	Low	High	High	High

Choosing the Right Client Hardware

A crucial aspect of your user's experience is the combination of applications they need to get their jobs done and the devices they use to make it happen. If you're asking, "What is the right hardware for my users?" the answer is a solid, "It depends."

The answers may vary depending on the user:

>> Is the user tethered to a desk or do they need something portable?

>> Do they need a device with a variety of inputs, such as keyboard, mouse, or touch — or do they simply need something that they can tap?

>> Does the user sometimes need to work offline, or are they always online and able to connect to the Internet?

>> Do users need more powerful CPU and GPU resources than those that their client hardware provides?

>> Do users need to collaborate with colleagues around the globe?

TIP

In Chapters 2-6, you learn more about VDI and DaaS, and the answer to the client question emerges.

Chapter **2**

What Is Virtual Desktop Infrastructure?

As Chapter 1 shows, virtual desktop infrastructure (VDI) emerged through an "Aha!" moment during which someone attempted to equate desktop workloads with server-based ones. This moment led to years of frustration as critical differences between server and desktop workloads revealed themselves and organizations struggled to develop virtual desktop architectures that carried a reasonable total cost of ownership (TCO).

VDI was — and still is — an incredibly promising technology, but it isn't necessarily for everyone, at least not in its traditional form. As VDI's shortcomings were solved with technology enhancements, more organizations discovered a positive technical and financial experience.

Still, though, VDI isn't for everyone. This chapter shows you what makes VDI tick and how you can overcome those pesky technical challenges that I discuss in Chapter 1.

Reviewing How VDI Works:
An Architectural View

Once a VDI environment is created, it's a wonderful thing. However, with some VDI solutions, getting from zero to desktops can be a heavy lift because a lot of parts have to come together just right to make it all happen.

VDI hardware elements

A traditional VDI deployment carries with it a lot of hardware requirements. At first glance, you may not think the hardware side should be all that complex, but as early VDI pilot failures demonstrated, too little attention to hardware in VDI can spell doom. Further, as specialized software permeates a desktop environment, that can pose hardware challenges in the VDI deployment as well.

Here are the components for which you'll need Visio stencils to develop your VDI architectural plans:

>> **Servers:** Like server virtualization, desktop virtualization requires host servers to host the virtual desktops.

>> **Storage:** Storage is important in both server and desktop virtualization environments, but used to be *the* limiting issue for VDI because of the way desktops operate in lockstep with one another. That's why the storage selected for a VDI environment is absolutely critical. **Hint:** With VDI, flash is a requirement, not just a nice-to-have.

>> **Network:** Rarely do organizations need or want single server VDI clusters, so having a network to connect multiple VDI hosts together is a nice touch. Moreover, in order for clients to connect to virtual desktops, a network is a relatively essential element.

>> **Graphics accelerators:** Some applications work just fine without video acceleration, but many don't. A number of tools in the application space require specialized graphics hardware to be able to work. This has traditionally been a difficult challenge to overcome in VDI environments, but more recent advancements have helped to overcome it.

Figure 2-1 shows what a VDI hardware environment might look like.

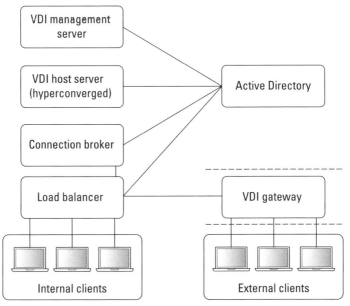

FIGURE 2-1: The components in a sample VDI hardware architecture.

HYPERCONVERGED INFRASTRUCTURE TO THE RESCUE!

Some of these elements are easily satisfied through the use of hyperconverged infrastructure. At its most basic, *hyperconverged infrastructure* is a data center architecture that eschews siloed storage and combines, at a minimum, storage, compute, and a hypervisor into a single software element that can run atop commodity server hardware. This technology has emerged as a leading method by which to get VDI done. At a minimum, a hyperconverged solution handily satisfied the servers and storage portions of VDI, and some solutions even include graphics accelerators to make sure that graphics-intensive applications can operate with ease in such environments.

Of course, in addition to server-side infrastructure, you need clients as well, but I talk about those later.

VDI software elements

The hardware needed in VDI is pretty straightforward. The software side can be either relatively simple for simple deployments or really complex if you design it that way. The following list is an overview of some of the common elements in a VDI scenario.

>> **Hypervisor:** First, of course, you need a hypervisor. That's a given in any solution that virtualizes entire systems.

>> **Connection broker:** You're likely operating multiple hosts with different pools of virtual desktops. You might have a pool of desktops for high performance needs and others that are configured for email. The connection broker provides a way for users to log in. From there, the broker software redirects the user to the right desktop pool.

>> **Load balancer:** Sometimes, the broker also provides load balancing services to make sure that user desktop workloads are evenly distributed among all of the hosts. This arrangement ensures that no one host is overwhelmed while others sit by twiddling their processors.

>> **Management server:** The management server provides a general administrative lens into the environment and is the method by which the individual virtual desktops are managed.

>> **Management agent:** Inside each managed desktop in a VDI environment is typically a software agent that allows the management server control over the operating system. This agent is the method by which the management server works its oversight magic.

>> **Application virtualization tool:** Application virtualization tools don't have to be used by themselves. They can be used with other desktop virtualization technologies, too. Sometimes you'll find them used in VDI environments to make application deployments easier.

>> **Client software:** Each device that will connect to the environment needs a client of some kind.

It might be easier to see a VDI diagram and how it might look when it's all done. So, take a look at Figure 2-2.

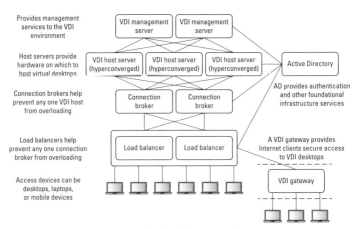

Provides management services to the VDI environment

Host servers provide hardware on which to host virtual desktops

Connection brokers help prevent any one VDI host from overloading

Load balancers help prevent any one connection broker from overloading

Access devices can be desktops, laptops, or mobile devices

VDI management server

VDI management server

VDI host server (hyperconverged)

VDI host server (hyperconverged)

VDI host server (hyperconverged)

Active Directory

AD provides authentication and other foundational infrastructure services

Connection broker

Connection broker

Load balancer

Load balancer

A VDI gateway provides Internet clients secure access to VDI desktops

VDI gateway

FIGURE 2-2: A fully built-out and redundant VDI architecture.

Understanding the Business and Technical Benefits of VDI

Now that you've gotten a look at the components that comprise a VDI environment, this section takes you on a journey down the road of benefits and helps you discover the treasures that can await you at the end of your VDI project. The benefits are many!

Becoming device agnostic

These days, a bunch of different device types litter the end-user computing landscape. You have desktops and laptops. You have Windows devices, Apple devices, and Linux devices. You have ultraportable laptops, tablets, and mini-tablets. You have smart phones. Heck, you even have smart watches.

Devices of all shapes, sizes, form factors, and operating systems are strewn about and your users want to use the one of their choice . . . or, in some cases, all of them! Suppose you tried to support, literally, every device on the planet in the same way that you supported a typical traditional desktop environment. Your life would descend into chaos and madness.

My advice: Avoid this fate!

VDI means that you deploy a single "gold master" virtual desktop and users simply consume copies of the master (a.k.a. non-persistent VMs) from any device that they want. Boom! Done. Now, your life is spent on a beach!

Enabling BYOD

For a decade, organizations have been adapting to bring-your-own-device (BYOD) trends. Users, as the name implies, bring their own devices to work and use them to get their work done. The organization might still subsidize the purchase of a device, but the user owns it, or, the company may provide a device but allow users to also use their own devices when necessary.

BYOD has a lot of benefits. Because employees often have their own computers, they can use what they already know. If they use a work computer at work, they don't need to drag it back and forth when they work from home.

In this context, VDI can be an incredible boon. Without it, that user would have two different devices with two sets of software installations to deal with. With VDI, the user simply connects to their central virtual desktop, no matter the device, and they get to have the exact same experience. If they're writing a report on their work computer, when they get home, they can simply reconnect to their VDI session and resume working on it without messing with copies of files.

It's a beautiful virtual world!

Discovering the security benefits of VDI

Chief information officers (CIOs) across the globe fretted over BYOD trends, developing policies to prevent what they were certain would destroy their carefully laid security barriers, represent the downfall of the entire *homo sapiens* species, and accelerate the end of the Earth itself by forcing the planet out of its orbit and directly into the Sun.

Since you're sitting in the comfort of your living room, your office, or a terrible Maroon 5 concert reading this book, it's safe to say that BYOD did not, in fact, destroy human civilization.

All kidding aside, CIOs were right to be concerned with what BYOD *could* represent, although some were a bit overzealous in their rejection of the trend. Without proper protocols in place, BYOD could have become a security and compliance nightmare. No longer would company data reside on devices controlled and managed by IT. Such data might reside alongside the kids' favorite games on a computer that didn't have a password and had helpfully labeled folders such as "Super-Secret and Valuable Work Data."

Even with encrypted devices, companies don't want to risk the loss of data. The downsides are fierce, including potential expense and reputational damage.

REMEMBER

VDI, however, handily solves the BYOD security nightmare. Users access their data through secure and encrypted clients. No data has to traverse that connection. All of the processing takes place on servers safely ensconced inside the walls of your data center. Again — *the user's data never leaves the data center.* If a device is lost or stolen, you simply give the user a new one and tell them to be more careful next time. The loss of a device doesn't induce a security incident.

Scaling VDI

In a traditional scenario, as you need more desktops, you go through a comprehensive deployment process in which your admins install the company's software or you image the machine. The process isn't too hard, but with many desktops, it can take a lot of time and it's inefficient.

In a VDI environment, as you need to scale, you simply add servers and make sure your users have an appropriate client to connect to the environment.

Determining Where VDI Presents Challenges

VDI can present a few challenges that need to be overcome.

Rethinking "desktops are just small servers"

Around the time server virtualization became red hot, someone thought, "Hmmm . . . desktops are just tiny little servers. Let's virtualize those bad boys, too!" Although they had the right idea, the reality was vastly different.

WARNING

Comparisons between server virtualization and virtual desktops should stop in their tracks. Desktops have proven to be very different animals. Server workloads perform very differently from desktops. Although there are performance peaks and valleys, server workloads exhibit more variance in these peaks and valleys, so a lot of workloads can easily share a physical server because those variances don't usually align between applications. Virtual desktops tend to perform in lockstep with one another at certain times of the day, resulting in a performance scenario that can pretty much destroy the host servers.

Consider, for example, a typical company. People often roll into the office in packs, with everyone arriving between, say, 7:30 and 9 a.m. You might see dozens of people attempting to log in to their desktops simultaneously. The result: a virtual desktop host that sees a serious spike in storage, CPU, and RAM utilization. In fact, this phenomenon has a couple of names — *boot storm* or *login storm*. Figure 2-3 gives you a look at this concept.

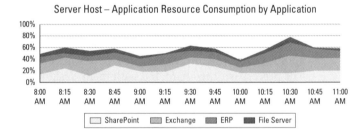

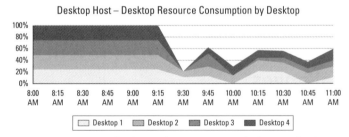

FIGURE 2-3: Server application performance versus desktop applications.

Early VDI deployments easily succumbed to these performance issues and were abandoned, which also made VDI look less attractive overall. Organizations worked hard to architect VDI environments that avoided this issue, but it was hard, at least until the advent of flash storage as a common storage medium. Although flash pretty handily solves the problem, people remembered VDI as having issues.

Traditional VDI presented other challenges as well, such as the performance of graphics-intensive applications. Early VDI implementations couldn't support these needs. The result was a disastrous user experience that was the second factor in dooming VDI for a while.

Refocusing economics

Even though the early days of VDI were tough challenges, people learned from those issues. VDI has resurged with new hardware and software that overcome the technical challenges that plagued early implementations. Perhaps the biggest downside for some organizations now is cost. VDI is a capital-intensive undertaking and requires the purchase of a significant amount of hardware. Additionally, it can still be complex from a management perspective. The result is often a need to hire people specially trained in and certified to build such environments because there are so many moving parts, including VDI hosts, brokers, gateways, and other components.

Frankly, in an IT market with a shrinking talent pool, it can be tough to find experts who know about all of these things. You may end up needing to work with outside consultants with such expertise, but the costs can add up quickly. As much as your typical IT department needs IT generalists for most activities today, some things, like VDI, still require specialized expertise.

REMEMBER

It's important to separate the software and hardware when talking about the economics. Even though early VDI efforts were challenges, modern ones work really, really well. The primary challenge there is cost. That huge purchase order that's needed to buy all of the hardware for the VDI environment can be substantial.

On the software front, it's mostly a question of calculating the licensing costs for the VDI environment and then adding it to the hardware cost to see if the new environment has a TCO that is less than the old desktop environment.

Overcoming On-Premises VDI Challenges

You have a couple of ways to deal with on-premises VDI challenges. On the hardware front, it's better to consider a simple hyperconverged solution than trying to build the environment yourself.

It's hard to "dip your toes" in the VDI water. In an all-in approach, you can reshape the desktop environment in a way that allows you to completely rethink the economics.

Another way to address the on-premises VDI challenges is to just not do it . . . but do desktop-as-a-service instead. That way, you're fully transferring those capital costs into a fixed monthly cost instead. You pay for only what you use and no more.

Chapter **3**

The Need for Change: Moving to the Cloud

You may have heard of the cloud. Apparently, it's big. Seriously, though, the cloud has completely reshaped everything about how we think about IT. Even if you're not doing anything with the cloud, you should consider two points. First, you're probably wrong; someone in your organization is working with the cloud. Second, there's incredible opportunity for you to meet your company's needs through the use of cloud services.

This chapter is your introduction to all things cloud. It shows you why companies are adopting the cloud and why it just might be the perfect place for you to operate your desktop computing environment.

Comparing and Contrasting Cloud Options

"The cloud" is a nebulous term. Get it? *Nebulous?* So many definitions are floating around out there that "cloud" has become almost a meaningless term that simply means "all of computing."

Of course, the situation isn't really quite that dire. This chapter provides some standard definitions for different types of cloud computing that will help to clarify your options.

Exploring the Public Cloud

Many public cloud options are available, from solutions such as AWS and Microsoft Azure to services such as Salesforce. You might be scratching your head a bit at the reference to Salesforce, but it is, in fact, in a cloud services category.

To begin, look at the full gamut of the stack that you need to consider as you're looking for a place to operate applications:

>> **Applications:** An application in this context is the user's entry point. It's the tool that the user directly leverages to make use of underlying data and services.

>> **Data:** This is the data that the application uses.

>> **Runtime:** The runtime layer supports an application while it is running.

>> **Middleware:** The middleware layer handles connectivity between systems and application to other infrastructure elements. Sometimes, middleware is used to help applications leverage resources not provided by the underlying operating system. Middleware is sometimes described as the plumbing that gets resources delivered from one place to another.

>> **Operating systems:** Operating systems are pretty self-explanatory. Think Windows, UNIX, or Linux.

>> **Virtualization layer:** The virtualization layer provides all of the abstraction necessary for the operating system to access shared underlying resources.

>> **Servers:** Servers provide the compute and memory services needed for the operating system to, well, operate. In a hyperconverged world, servers also provide the storage and, sometimes, the networking components.

>> **Storage:** You already know what storage is!

>> **Networking:** You also know what networks are.

You might be wondering why I bothered to list these resources. Here's why: As you consider the cloud options at your disposal, you will find that each one provides a different set of capabilities, all based around the elements in the preceding list. In general, three public cloud models exist:

>> **Infrastructure-as-a-service (IaaS):** In this model, the provider gives you everything up to and including the virtualization layer. From there, you manage the rest. Examples include Microsoft Azure, AWS, and Google Compute Engine, among many others.

>> **Platform-as-a-service (PaaS):** In PaaS, you only have to worry about the data and applications. The provider takes care of everything else. Nutanix's Frame desktop-as-a-service offering falls here.

>> **Software-as-a-service (SaaS):** With SaaS, the provider does it all and you just consume the service. Examples include Salesforce and Office 365.

Figure 3-1 provides a visual comparison matrix for these three primary cloud delivery models.

	IaaS	PaaS	SaaS
Applications	You manage	You manage	Provider manages
Data	You manage	You manage	Provider manages
Runtime	You manage	Provider manages	Provider manages
Middleware	You manage	Provider manages	Provider manages
OS	You manage	Provider manages	Provider manages
Virtualization	Provider manages	Provider manages	Provider manages
Servers	Provider manages	Provider manages	Provider manages
Storage	Provider manages	Provider manages	Provider manages
Networking	Provider manages	Provider manages	Provider manages

FIGURE 3-1: Primary public cloud delivery models.

Finding Out Why Organizations Are Making the Public Cloud Jump

Even though the world is a decade into the cloud era, organizations of all shapes and sizes are still considering what move, if any, they want to make with regard to the cloud. So, it makes sense to look at what the cloud offers.

Introducing cloud economics

Let's say you're in the market for a car. You know that you plan to keep the car for up to five years. You also know that your in-laws are moving to town and you need something big enough to haul you, your spouse, your two kids, and your in-laws to work, to school, and to and from doctors' appointments. Your job is pretty close to home, so you're not too worried about gas mileage.

Based on your best projections, you need a car that seats at least six and mileage is not a big concern. Based on that set of criteria, you walk into a dealership, hand them a stack of cash, and leave with the car.

Nice job! You now own a car.

The day after you leave the dealership, your in-laws call you to let you know that they've decided to stay with their other kid and won't be moving to your town. The next phone call is from your boss to let you know that the company is transferring you to an office that is a 45-minute commute away.

Suddenly you have a too-large vehicle that gets too-low mileage for your needs, and you own it. Buying data center equipment can work the same way. You do your best to plan ahead, but you don't always get it right and you're stuck with your purchase until the next replacement cycle.

REMEMBER

With a traditional data center procurement model, you buy everything up front — a serious capital expenditure — use it for as long as you can, and then throw it all away and begin anew with then-current equipment. It's a wasteful model. If something unexpected happens in the middle of the cycle, you're left scrambling to figure out the budget and operational impact.

GOODBYE, DATA CENTER?

You may be thinking that a cloud adoption process involves your company sending checks to a cloud service provider and then taking sledgehammers into the data center and "carefully removing" the equipment you just stopped using. Reality is a tad different. With some exceptions, organizations aren't throwing everything into the public cloud. They are retaining on-premises data centers that operate in conjunction with their public cloud deployments, creating what has become known as a *hybrid cloud*. Public cloud adoption has certainly had an impact on enterprise IT vendors, but the fact is that companies are still building data centers.

A cloud economic model allows you to adopt a pay-as-you-go mentality. You buy what you need today. When you need more, you buy more.

With the cloud, you have no capital costs directly applied by the cloud service provider. Everything is an operational expense. Rather than driving a truckload of money to an enterprise IT vendor, you're essentially paying a rent check each month to a cloud service provider.

The immediacy factor

What's your process for buying more storage capacity in your current data center? You likely have a series of approval processes you have to go through after which a purchase order is cut and then you wait for the new equipment to arrive on your dock. Next, you spend some time racking and cabling the new storage and you then go through whatever deployment process is required by the vendor.

The setup isn't likely to be all that involved from a technical perspective, but it can take weeks to months to complete because of the nature of decision-making and the realities of the shipping process.

If you needed that capacity right now, you'd be in a bind, wouldn't you?

With the public cloud, the procurement and deployment process consists of logging in to the cloud provider's management portal and clicking a few buttons. Within seconds, you have that extra storage that you so desperately need. Of course, your next monthly invoice will reflect the fact that you just asked for more services.

Elevating IT operations to strategy versus tactics

One challenge that has faced IT organizations for decades is one of bifurcated priorities. On one hand, organizations need to make sure that there's someone keeping the lights on in the data center, but on the other, they need someone to help guide them on their path to digital prosperity.

IT departments and CIOs are expected to do both. Unfortunately, the focus has too often been on the ongoing tactical needs of the organization rather than on strategy. The result is a constant onslaught of bloggers lamenting the IT/business divide and talking about how out of touch CIOs are because they have to focus on tactics.

REMEMBER

Although CIOs really do need to focus more on strategy than tactics, the products and services that they've deployed into the data center have often worked against them. Data centers have traditionally been complex beasts to wrangle and CIOs have had to build teams of people to manage each individual component. The CIOs then have had to make sure that those teams work together to support a complete operating environment for the organization.

Although some technologies, such as hyperconverged infrastructure, have had a dramatic impact on righting the data center ship, what would life be like if there were, in fact, no infrastructure to manage? You'd still need someone to turn dials to ramp resources up and down and to pull together the right cloud services to make everything work, but you wouldn't need dozens of people on the payroll to create storage logical unit numbers (LUNs), for example.

Such a move would probably allow you and your company to focus more on overall strategy than on the mechanics of keeping it all running, especially as more companies undertake digital transformation efforts. With this point in mind, as you consider your future technology efforts, whether they're around server-side computing or desktop computing, don't forget to consider how the public cloud might be able to help you execute on a strategy.

DON'T FORGET PRIVATE CLOUD!

In all this talk about the public cloud, you can easily forget that there is a flip side to the cloud coin — private clouds. In the simplest terms, private clouds are on-premises data centers that operate similarly to public clouds. The public cloud can be a compelling location in which to operate workloads, but it can have serious downsides as well. Some applications simply can't run in the public cloud or you may have discovered that public cloud economic benefits don't hold true for your particular use case.

However, you still may be able to have a public cloud-like experience. It takes rethinking how you operate the on-premises environment. You can't simply virtualize everything and then declare, "I am now a private cloud!" You need a management and orchestration layer that brings to your environment the kinds of management capabilities that are inherent in public cloud.

By making the investment necessary to bring your data center to private cloud standards, you can enjoy some of the benefits of the public cloud while retaining the control you currently have over your infrastructure.

Your private cloud environment is increasingly likely to be part of an overall suite of cloud services that you deploy. Many organizations are augmenting their private cloud environments with services from multiple cloud providers, thus creating *multi-cloud* environments. Organizations leveraging multi-cloud services choose which services they want from which cloud, providing their organizations with a great deal of flexibility when it comes to new service deployment.

Considering the Reasons for Desktops in the Cloud

You may be wondering — rightly — what the cloud has to do with desktops. This is where the rubber hits the road. Believe it or not, your desktop environment may be a prime candidate for cloudification, and you may find that you get the benefits that I discuss in the preceding sections.

You have many reasons to consider desktops in the cloud:

>> **No more local VDI:** You don't need to deal with all those moving parts.

>> **On-demand:** Hiring a new employee? Her desktop is provisioned and she can use the laptop she brought with her.

>> **Pay as you go:** Pay for just what you're using and nothing more.

>> **Reduced CapEx:** You don't need to buy a bunch of stuff up front to make this all happen.

>> **A strategic focus:** Rather than spending your time on tactical desktop operations, you can be focusing on company strategy.

TIP

Chapters 4 and 5 dive deeply into desktop-as-a-service.

Chapter **4**

Understanding Desktop-as-a-Service

And now, the moment you've been waiting for! As technology is wont to do, it's leaping ahead, and that includes the desktop space.

Virtual desktop infrastructure (VDI) has been a powerful participant in the desktop discussion but has also been prophetically problematic along the way. In this chapter, you discover how the newest entrant in the desktop diatribe delivers results for organizations and how it can help your company as it seeks to undertake a renewed digital journey.

Without further ado, here's desktop-as-a-service (DaaS).

Finding a Simpler Desktop Deployment Service: DaaS

I talk in Chapter 2 about the difficulty in supporting a traditional desktop model. I explain in Chapter 3 how a traditional IT procurement model is financially inefficient because it requires boats full of cash making an end run around the border wall.

DaaS: PUBLIC OR PRIVATE CLOUD?

In most cases, DaaS services operate in the public cloud, but you can think about DaaS in a private cloud environment as well. In this case, the virtual desktops are housed in your data center and consumed from there. Nearly everything else, though, stays the same. You still pay the DaaS vendor a monthly fee for the DaaS management service that is still hosted in the cloud. You still manage everything through the same web-based console. Users still access their virtual desktops from anywhere on any device. Although you buy some infrastructure for your data center, you still get the benefits of the "cloudiness" of the solution. Right now, you have to look hard to find a true private cloud DaaS solution, but I predict that to be a situation that will change very soon.

DaaS is here to fix all of this in one fell swoop.

First, consider DaaS from a high level. What, exactly, is it? DaaS is a method by which desktop computers are operated fully in the cloud.

From an operational perspective, DaaS effectively mimics the user benefits that you see in VDI or with other server-based desktop technologies. However, you don't need to have a team of dedicated IT staff to make it all work. That's the job of the provider.

REMEMBER

From the get-go, DaaS is about simplicity. It's about simplicity for IT as well as for the user. For IT, you don't have to throw a bunch of new gear into the data center, and for users, if you have the right DaaS solution, you need nothing more than a browser that supports HTML5.

Gaining Perspective: How DaaS Differs from VDI

At first, you may wonder what VDI and DaaS have in common and, more importantly, what they *don't* have in common. The first is obvious. VDI is a service that you build and manage directly, whether that means it operates solely within the four walls of your data center, or you build it on a public cloud provider. DaaS operates across the globe in secured data centers operated by cloud providers while the DaaS service itself is managed by your vendor.

The client side is also potentially different, but in a good way. DaaS typically needs nothing more than an HTML5-equipped web browser to operate. With VDI, there's usually a dedicated client to worry about. Of course, good VDI software makes it possible to use just HTML5, but that requires additional setup and configuration by IT. It isn't generally an out-of-the-box experience.

Not everything is roses with DaaS, though. Suppose you're at your desk in the office working away and the connection to the Internet goes down. The impact on you is low because your desktop is operating in a room just down the hall. If your desktop is operating in a different location, of course, you're dead in the water.

With DaaS, if the Internet decides to take a break to watch cat memes, you're definitely out of luck because DaaS requires a working connection to the Internet.

On the overall reliability front, DaaS has the upper hand, in most cases. DaaS providers stake their business on making sure that desktops work and, with that singular mind-set, that's all they do. Your internal IT team may be wonderful, but they have other jobs to do that may not make them as fast on the uptake at correcting a problem when it arises. Table 4-1 provides a quick comparison matrix between VDI and DaaS.

TABLE 4-1 **The VDI versus DaaS Smackdown**

	VDI	DaaS
Deployment (IT)	A heavy lift	Done between episodes of *Star Trek*
End-user Experience	Depends on what IT allows	HTML5 browser and you're off!
Networking Needs	Depends; the intranet may still work even if the Internet is down	If the Internet is down, so are you
Reliability	Depends on how good your IT is	SLA-driven

Swapping CapEx for OpEx with DaaS

There are some financial elements to consider when you compare DaaS to other desktop technologies. DaaS is a cloud service and carries with it the cloud economic model discussed in Chapter 3. VDI carries with it a CapEx-centric operating model.

With DaaS, you may not ultimately pay *less* than you do for VDI, but you will pay *differently*. Ultimately, with a DaaS environment, you're swapping the CapEx for VDI with an OpEx expenditure.

That trade may not sound like it has a financial benefit, but it does. First, you're only paying for what you use. If, midyear, your company decides to shed half its staff, you aren't left holding the VDI bag that's now twice as big as it needs to be. You can simply call the DaaS provider and let them know that you need to dial things down a bit.

Further, as I mention in Chapter 3, by not having to focus on a complex VDI environment full of hosts, brokers, and gateways, you might be able to get a stronger strategic foothold in your company.

Appreciating On-Demand Desktop Scaling Elasticity

Finally, consider scale. The previous example talks about losing half your staff. What if the opposite happens? What if your company quickly doubles the size of its workforce? You're constantly on the hook for growing that VDI environment by leaps and bounds and you may fall behind, leaving new employees without a desktop environment.

With DaaS, the number of people you hire doesn't matter. You just click "Add User" each time a new, signed offer letter comes back and you've provisioned a desktop for that new employee.

Moreover, if you discover that a whole department needs its desktops to be beefier, you don't have to worry about any limits imposed by how much hardware you have on-site. You can simply reconfigure the desktops in the DaaS provider's console to grant that department the resources it needs.

Chapter **5**

Adopting DaaS

D aaS is a desktop in the cloud. It sounds so very simple. Frankly, it is, but that doesn't mean you don't have home- work to do. After all, your current desktop operating envi- ronment is hardly the picture of uniformity. Your DaaS environment will likely have some non-uniform needs that you need to take into consideration as well.

In this chapter, you learn what steps you need to take once you've made the decision to adopt DaaS to serve your company's desktop needs.

Choosing a Desktop Deployment Method: The Decision Matrix

You have a lot of options when it comes to desktop deployment models. In Chapter 1, I talk about the options you have at your disposal. Those options don't go away just because DaaS is on the scene now. You just have another option now when it comes to the decision criteria.

Much like a certain brand-name potato chip, you don't need to limit yourself to just one model. You may choose to keep a traditional desktop or laptop model for your road warriors and those who need a lot of custom applications, and use DaaS for everyone else.

Figure 5-1 provides a decision matrix to help you decide which model makes the most sense when.

	Traditional Desktops	DaaS	VDI
Personas			
IT staff	●	○	○
Road warrior	●	●	●
Power user	●	●	●
Light user/transactional user	○	●	●
Situations			
Situation: Need a desktop *now*	✕	●	●
Require 100 percent desktop availability, even without a network	●	✕	✕
Have a dedicated desktop team	●	●	●
No dedicated desktop team	○	●	✕
Require simplicity	○	●	✕
Economics			
Need an OpEx model	✕	●	✕
Prefer a CapEx model	●	✕	●

● Good solution   ○ May work — situational   ✕ Not recommended

FIGURE 5-1: A traditional versus DaaS versus VDI deployment decision matrix.

Identifying Differences Between On-Premises and Cloud DaaS

DaaS is a born-in-the-cloud service, but that doesn't mean that it's restricted to *only* the public cloud. It's possible to operate DaaS using an on-premises deployment instead. For example, you may work for an organization that requires end-to-end control of the computing experience for your users because of security or compliance concerns, or you may work for a company that prefers to house its own equipment.

As you consider on-premises DaaS versus cloud DaaS, what differences emerge? Table 5-1 shows you.

TABLE 5-1 On-Premises versus Cloud DaaS

	On-premises DaaS	Cloud DaaS
Who supports?	Provider or IT	Provider
Cost model	Pay monthly per desktop	Pay monthly per desktop
Hardware purchase needed	Servers for the virtual desktops and underlying networking	None
Scaling latency	Moderate (new hardware must be shipped)	None
Reliability	Dependent on your environment	Guaranteed via an SLA

From a user perspective and from the perspective of the person in IT who manages the DaaS environment, an on-premises DaaS solution operates either identically or very close to the cloud solution. Both use the same management interface and tools.

However, the on-premises DaaS solution may have some challenges to overcome. Most importantly, your IT department will manage some aspects of the environment that typically would be handled by the service provider. Even though the service provider likely will provide support for the service itself, IT will have to ensure that power, networking, cooling, and other underlying data center services are provided to the DaaS servers. Even if the provider sends an all-in-one cabinet that contains all of the networking needed for the solution, IT still has to connect that to the network. That process involves making sure there is appropriate IP addressing, firewalling, and more.

TIP

When it comes time to add capacity to the DaaS environment, you need to wait for the provider to ship you new hardware. However, it's more than likely that the provider implemented some level of capacity management, so they may be able to get you hardware before you even know you need it. I recommend that you work with the provider to see what they can do for you.

In essence, when you buy the cloud-based DaaS, you're buying a service that is ready to go as soon as you provide a credit card number. With an on-premises DaaS environment, a little more work will be involved for IT.

There's one huge BUT here. No matter what, with either on-premises DaaS or cloud DaaS, you don't need an IT skill set that involves VDI. The provider will handle all aspects of that for you.

Making the Case for DaaS

DaaS is clearly a departure from what many organizations are used to. That's partially why you need to consider it. Change *can* be a good thing! As with many other things, though, decision-makers need proper justification for an undertaking.

Here is a laundry list of justification items that you can use to get from "Hmmm" to "YES! DO IT NOW!" from decision-makers:

>> **You can kick the tires.** With VDI, testing in a full production capacity can be difficult. Projects take a long time to get going. Sure, you can do proofs of concept with a subset of the final solution, but you can't *really* test it unless you're running at full tilt, and that incudes under load. With DaaS, you get to kick the tires without making a huge capital commitment ahead of time.

>> **You can scale from one to thousands on a whim.** Do you need just one virtual desktop? That would be pretty foolish to run on a complete VDI deployment. Do you need thousands? That would require a ton of new hardware and internal IT expertise if you do it on VDI. With DaaS, you can start small and scale bigger as needed.

>> **Your monthly invoice is for only what you use.** VDI requires a heavy upfront investment. DaaS turns your desktop environment into a monthly invoice.

>> **Bring on BYOD.** If you're operating a traditional desktop model now but your users are clamoring for BYOD, DaaS is just what the CIO ordered. You can kickstart that BYOD initiative without worrying that your desktop environment will wreak havoc on everything else.

>> **Implementation takes minutes, not weeks or months.** If you're considering VDI, you're in for what can be a complex road with specialized servers and a specialized skill set. With DaaS, you can jumpstart your virtual desktop program in minutes, getting up and running far more quickly than other options can enable.

- >> **Management is simple.** Point and click here. Tap there. Managing DaaS means that you focus on what your end-users need, not on a bunch of complex infrastructure elements that the users never see.

- >> **You don't need specialized skills.** Because the underlying complexity is abstracted away by the provider, you don't need to hire VDI gurus. Instead, you get to work with your users on solving their needs.

- >> **Your desktop data is instantly secured.** If you have a bunch of laptop-toting users storing data locally, especially if those devices aren't encrypted, you're staring down the barrel of a disaster waiting to happen. DaaS instantly solves that problem. All user data resides in the data center or the provider's protected walls and never leaves those confines unless you specifically allow it to.

- >> **It's location-independent.** Even if you give every one of your users a laptop, it isn't on 24/7. With a DaaS environment, you can more easily interrupt an employee's wedding with a vital request that they can fulfill using an HTML5-laden browser from any device. The person to whom you've made the request will surely thank you for how easy you've made it!

Considering Options: Key Features to Consider

As you seek DaaS as a potential addition to your IT services port-folio, look for these critical features:

- >> **Multi-level account structure:** Does the solution provide an account structure that allows you to start small and grow bigger by enabling other administrators to handle routine tasks while you manage who is allowed to use those admin accounts?

- >> **Integrated metering and billing:** Like any cloud solution, you should only pay for what you use in a DaaS environment. That's one of the key economic benefits of the public cloud. Does the DaaS solution you're considering include integrated metering and billing so that you can sleep at night knowing that you're not being overbilled or paying for resources that sit idle?

- **API integration:** Software-defined infrastructure is eminently programmable, a feature that should carry over to your desktop environment. Can your solution allow you to seamlessly embed applications inside web pages? Can it allow you to automatically publish a new desktop for a newly hired employee?

- **Elastic infrastructure:** Does the solution allow you to grow and, just as importantly, shrink the environment on-demand and without penalty? You may have seasonal needs that you need to satisfy, so it's important that your DaaS solution be able to accommodate these needs without costing you money. As a part of this, can individual desktops grow on-demand to accommodate new user needs?

- **Application catalog.** Does the solution provide an easy-to-use catalog from which admins and/or users can choose applications to enable in their desktop environment? The easier it is for your users to get their work done, the happier they will be with the environment.

- **Cloud storage support:** Are you a Dropbox user? Maybe OneDrive or Google Drive? Does the solution you're considering support the file-sharing application you currently use?

- **Browser-based client:** Everyone has a web browser. Your DaaS vendor's solution should be accessible using any browser rather than relying on a custom application that may or may not be available to all of your users wherever they find themselves.

- **Your choice of cloud:** Does the DaaS provider you're considering force you into Amazon when you're already heavily invested in Azure, or vice versa? Make sure that your DaaS provider's solution allows you to use the cloud of your choice and to switch cloud providers if you find it necessary to do so.

Choosing the Right Client Hardware

This section is almost laughably easy to write, dear reader. The right client hardware = any device with an HTML5–capable browser or, in other words, any modern device.

Oh, I guess there is a little more. With DaaS, the client you choose is really one of form factor, not speeds and feeds. Even the tiniest of laptops can get the job done, if necessary. With a DaaS deployment, right-sizing the client is a matter of focusing on screen size and input device, not CPU, RAM, or storage configuration.

That's refreshing, really. You no longer need to buy devices that have multi-terabytes of flash because all data is stored on the hosted desktop.

TIP

Work with your users to determine if they prefer a desktop computer, a laptop or even a tablet. Provide them with dual screens, if that's what they need.

For some devices for which an HTML5 browser may not be readily available — such as some tablets or phones — the device manufacturer's app store typically has a compatible client.

Right-Sizing Desktops

There's a reason that you have a fleet of desktops with a wildly varying configuration landscape. That reason: Different users have different needs. Adopting DaaS doesn't change this fundamental fact. You still need to make sure that users can run the applications they need.

In other words, you need to *right-size* their desktops.

In a traditional environment, changing a user's desktop hardware configuration might mean tearing open the chassis and throwing in a stick of random access memory (RAM) here or a solid-state drive (SSD) there. Fortunately, with a DaaS environment, changing a desktop's hardware specs is a bit easier. You just log in to the DaaS portal and add more resources. No screwdriver is needed.

TECHNICAL
STUFF

For example, suppose you have a user who started as a billing clerk and had light needs. They might have been assigned a desktop with 8GB of RAM and a single CPU core. Today, that user has been shifted into a video editing job. Now, they need more, so you upgrade their desktop to one that sports 64GB of RAM, 16 cores of CPU, and 4 GPUs.

Wait . . . GPUs?

Adding 3D: Implementing DaaS That Supports High-End Graphics

The earliest incarnations of VDI had a critical flaw. The video experience for users was sub-optimal (it was terrible). Even watching a YouTube video was an exercise in frustration because it worked incredibly poorly. Users rejected the technology.

Over the years, various protocols were invented to help address this issue. Specialized protocols helped users with the graphics problem, but they required that you use both hardware and software that specifically worked with the technology.

That left VDI in the cold for many high-end needs.

REMEMBER

As you might guess, DaaS solves this problem. In fact, the right DaaS solution can harness the power of multiple GPUs and bring them to bear to allow even video rendering tasks to be accomplished in the DaaS workspace.

This capability to address the needs of 3D work and other ultra-high-end graphics work means that DaaS can handily run the application gamut. You can have task workers who just use it for email and you can have your entire CAD team using it for graphics-intensive work, all without having to build an ounce of infrastructure.

And they can do it from an iPad.

Adding Applications to Your DaaS Environment

You might wonder just how far a provider will let you go in terms of adding software to your DaaS environment. The answer *should* be: as far as you need, within the confines of application compatibility. You shouldn't expect that the DaaS environment will support Lotus 123 from the 1980s, no matter how badly you need it.

With a DaaS environment, you create an application catalog. To get applications into the catalog, you onboard those applications, which involves running through a single installation process, and then you make that application available to your users.

With some DaaS solutions, you can publish just a series of applications or you can allow users to have a full desktop, just as if they were sitting at a PC. What you decide to make available to your users is up to you and the needs of those users.

Accessing Users Files in DaaS

Here's another area where DaaS can shine. Your company might have an Internet connection that is good, but not great. That means that tools like Dropbox, Box, and Google Drive can be useful, but the time they take to synchronize files is high. To avoid that sync time, you might choose to sync everything.

What if you didn't have to?

What if you had a massive pipe from your desktop right to Dropbox? The right DaaS vendor provides exactly that. Their services are hosted on infrastructure with the largest pipes so your access to things like Dropbox will be practically instantaneous. Once you connect your file-sharing account to your DaaS service, you can access those files as if they were local.

Achieving Disaster Recovery in a DaaS World

Suppose you have a desktop and your company's building burns to the ground. That's going to be a bad day for your company and it may be days or weeks before you have a working desktop again.

Now, assume your company decided to adopt VDI. You could get up and running again pretty quickly, but what happens if the VDI environment burns to the ground? Unless your company implemented a mirror or distributed environment, you'll be down again.

With a DaaS provider, you no longer depend on a single site. With distributed operations, a DaaS provider can withstand the loss of one of their own sites and keep you operational. Best of all, it's all included in your monthly fee. You don't need to go through the expense and challenge of setting up your own DR services.

Chapter **6**

Ten Reasons Why DaaS Is the Future

t's time to discuss ten reasons why DaaS is so important to IT starting *today*:

» **Eliminating desktops (well . . .):** What if you could eliminate desktops from your environment? And laptops?

It likely won't fully happen in the very near future because current practices are so entrenched, but DaaS helps get you one step further. With DaaS, you don't need the localized processing power of a desktop or laptop and your users can use other devices. Alternatively, they can use stripped down, much lower-cost devices like Chromebooks because the heavy lifting is happening in the provider's environment.

» **No more VDI:** Traditional VDI is good, but not great, and it carries with it a lot of baggage. Cloud-based DaaS can help you fully jettison VDI from your data center. Even on-premises DaaS eschews VDI because the provider handles the hard parts of the desktop equation, leaving you to focus on application enablement.

» **A focus on strategy over tactics:** Do I smell a successful digital transformation in your future now that you can focus on strategy rather than tactics? DaaS is strategic. You focus on your

FRA.ME/TEST-DRIVE

user's outcomes rather than the underlying infrastructure. In fact, this is exactly what the future of IT needs to be in many areas, not just desktops.

» **Geographic limitations are shredded:** With DaaS, you can work quite literally, from anywhere with an Internet connection. Yes, you can do this with VDI as well.

Consider international travelers. News stories frequently mention issues at the border with cautions to wipe devices upon reentry into the country. What if there were no data at all to worry about? Your users carry a tablet or small laptop with them that has just a web browser.

» **BYOD is fully supported:** A DaaS deployment is a key step in allowing a BYOD program in the workplace. Why? Because it doesn't matter what else is happening on the user's device. All of the real work is happening in the provider's environment, which is safely isolated from the other software running on the device.

» **No more massive capital expenditures:** A VDI deployment may be preferable for some organizations, but, regardless, it requires a capital outlay for the server hosts and storage needed for the deployment. DaaS eliminates the need for a capital outlay in exchange for an operating expense in the form of a monthly payment.

» **Just pay a monthly invoice:** You trade CapEx for OpEx and only pay for what you actually use. That's the key to IT of the future. Why pay for what you're not using?

By the way, not all DaaS providers are equal. Some force you to sign up for a minimum subscription term. Be careful as you're choosing options.

» **Super-simple scalability:** As you add employees, you just provision new desktops for them using your DaaS provider's console. You don't ever hit a scaling wall. Even with VDI, at some point, you're going to hit the point at which you need to add more hardware to your environment. That never happens with DaaS.

» **Full control:** DaaS and BYOD don't mean that you lose total control of the environment. In fact, you may even *gain* control, depending on how you set it up. You get to decide which users get which applications.

» **Stepped-up security:** I'm saving the best for last. This is important now and will be even more important in the future. With DaaS, your desktop data never makes its way to porous devices that can leak data everywhere. It stays safely enshrined in the provider's data center.